STOCKPILE HEAVENLY TREASURES

PHILIP JOY

Trilogy Christian Publishers

A Wholly Owned Subsidiary of Trinity Broadcasting Network

2442 Michelle Drive

Tustin, CA 92780

For information, address Trilogy Christian Publishing

Rights Department, 2442 Michelle Drive, Tustin, Ca 92780.

Trilogy Christian Publishing/ TBN and colophon are trademarks of Trinity Broadcasting Network.

For information about special discounts for bulk purchases, please contact Trilogy Christian Publishing.

Manufactured in the United States of America

10 9 8 7 6 5 4 3 2 1

Library of Congress Cataloging-in-Publication Data is available.

ISBN 978-1-63769-198-4

ISBN 978-1-63769-199-1

FOREWORD

This book, *Stockpile Heavenly Treasures*, is about investing in God's kingdom. I started as an unlikely investor. I am a man who was attracted to men. Waking up to hope and grace on Trinity Broadcasting Network (TBN) changed my mind. I am no longer preoccupied with the number of days I have been pure. My focus is now Jesus. I tune in to the gentle voice of the Spirit that leads me to make investments in the Kingdom of God in various ways. It is easy to drown in shame for years when facing multiple storms like mine. I believe my book will help my readers go to the next level on their spiritual journeys. If a chief of sinners can do it in Christ, you can too!

I neither participate in nor condone gay life, but I love everyone equally as God does. He sent His Son to die on the cross for us all, even while we were in sin. The Creator infused gender identity assurance in the Garden of Eden. After I got saved, I had the zeal to honor my soul's love, Jesus, with my body but lacked knowledge. Without knowledge, people perish. I started watching more football and less theatrical performances to have an assurance of my gender identity. I went hunting, fishing, and Jeep off-roading. My lack of ease in my masculine identity was atoned for a while, only to multiply seven times later as I relied on my flesh. My attraction to men became out of control. My spirit was saved, but my soul was starving. My turning point into complete, lasting freedom was a simple act of chewing. For me, delivery into the first garden had two wings: comfort in my masculine identity and a new heterosexual orientation like the first couple.

What happened in the Garden of Eden with gender identity assurance can happen again and remain forever (Psalm 1:2–3). Adam had no doubt of his gender identity as a provider before the fall. He did not work long hours to provide for his family. The first man took care of the garden joyfully and had a lot of fun with his wife, multiplying and filling the earth. He derived his gender identity assurance by looking to his Maker as the provider.

Stressful work started to happen after the fall. Adam chewed on the fruit of good and evil. He left Eden and had no choice but to define his identity by the sweat of his brow. He started hunting, fishing, and tilling the land to paint a masculine flesh decaying with time. In the first psalm, the author described the righteous as a tree replanted in Eden's garden chewing on Scripture. Whether you consider yourself gay, lesbian, transgender, straight, or confused, you will probably enjoy a relocation to paradise in Eden. God is willing and able to replant you in Eden to flourish, never dropping a leaf. His promise in the first psalm is unshakable and irreversible. When will God replant you in Eden like He did for me? How do you chew on Scripture like I do to fill up your soul's belly? I am with you in the Spirit. Let's turn the page together to Chapter 1.

CHAPTER 1

TICKET TO HEAVEN

How do I repent? I can't! Loneliness was eating me alive, and I was hungry for love. I loved singing in church. Worship took me out of this world into a new one. I was scared to make friends. What if they knew? What if they noticed how I walk, shake my bonbons, or hold a drink with a raised pinky finger? I carefully hid my Streisand collection. People. People who need people are the most beautiful in the world. I turned to those melodies in my closet for comfort.

I was walking far away from everyone, and my soul was crying, "Unclean!" Not being able to talk to anyone about the love that does not dare speak its name, I dived into books. Some said to go be happy and live your life. Some said to stay single. I was swinging from one doctrine to another.

Heaven seemed unreachable. I watched all my friends get girlfriends and wives later on. Yet my miracle never arrived. I got married to a woman hoping against hope that I could give her intimacy. She knew while we were dating, yet she took the challenge.

I wanted to repent and become perfect in the eyes of God, so I started working on perfecting myself. Year after year, repentance seemed impossible. After church or an intense Bible reading, I was ready to promise, filled with the Word. I promised, alright. I would never again have a hookup or go to certain places online and offline. My first wife divorced me. I begged her to stay, but I was left home alone with no one to hug except the walls.

I needed a hug—only a hug, or so I thought. The desire to be loved led me to do way more. After the fact, shame visited me and made me lonelier than before. I was swinging between short, intense intimacy and shame. I tried, but I could never stop loving Jesus, and I never stopped believing that He is on my side after all these big mistakes (Matthew 10:8).

I was eating daily from the tree of good and evil. It made me sin-conscious instead of Jesus-conscious. The good I did was for my own good, and I didn't care about anyone else. I stopped all the research that brought more confusion and decided to walk with my Maker in the cool of the day, just like Adam before he got close to that cursed tree.

Jesus became a curse on the wooden cross. Just like me, you may feel like you are too far from heaven. Just like me, you may feel you are ready to quit repenting. My trials had been leading to errors for years, and I decided it was time to stop relying on my own effort to get out of my predicaments.

Confession of sins is essential for the believer. It is

a discussion with God so He can reveal the root cause of a particular sin, so we don't do it again. That root cause can vary from believer to believer. For example, at 250 pounds with back problems, I confessed my sin of gluttony. I was expecting that His Word would be a "Keto diet." It was not. It may be for others. For me it was changing my plan and cancelling some meetings to prevent overeating and to ease the stress. Confession does not erase the guilty stains. Only the blood of Jesus will pay for my sins and eliminate my guilt. Eating well will erase my back pain.

Cursed is He who hangs on a tree (Deuteronomy 21:23). Jesus will take our place if we let Him. Would you? I did. I simply stopped trying. I stopped condemning myself and stopped talking to anyone who criticized me. Not tomorrow. Not when I can pay the bills. Not when I can find another church to call home. If Jesus does not condemn me, no one can.

I told Jesus to come into my heart, and I will make Him my Lord and Savior. You tell Him. Invite Him into your heart too. You cannot be worse than the chief of sinners—me.

The blood of Christ covers your sins—past, present, and future. The essence of repentance is that God is for me and not against me. Will you change? No! Will He change you whenever He decides to? Yes! A change from self-effort will last a few days. An effortless change by the power invested in me from Jesus will happen by accident. I look, and my addiction has evaporated.

Is there room for confession? Why do we need it? Grace does not cancel the confession of sins but sheds light on its definition. Only the blood of Christ is a valid currency for sin payments. We confess in a guilt-free discussion with our Daddy God the best next step. Confession is essential for daily living because who else can have a better next step? For example, I was frequenting a particular establishment where people meet and greet and sometimes take a complete stranger home at the end of the night. I had formed amazing friendships there, and people were very loving and friendly—absolutely no condemnation. Many of my friends did not take anyone home, and this is not their point of weakness. It was mine. God led me to maintain those friendships over lunch and not in a nightclub. I learned not to trust my flesh and created boundaries.

Quit going to the tree of good and evil. It will kill you (Genesis 2:17). Just walk with Him in the cool of the garden. Open your ears to His gentle whisper. He will not ask you to wear a purity ring. He wants you to focus on His holiness, so you become precisely like Him as time goes by without even trying. He will not overwhelm you. He may simply guide you to a great place to eat and enjoy breakfast. He cooked fish for his disciples on the shores of the Sea of Galilee. He may suggest pancakes and bacon. It does not have to be kosher. You are no longer hanging out by that poisonous tree. You are with Jesus, the friend of sinners! One step at a time. One day at a time. He will change some of your desires and give you the power to execute the next step. He lifts you when you fall and teaches you to walk on better ground. He will take away the people who hurt you. He will bring people who build you up.

I don't have a ticket to heaven. I was looking for one most of my life. Time to stop! Heaven is now on earth. The joy of the companionship of Jesus is here on earth as it is in heaven. Even when I mess up, I don't care anymore. The more I get to know Him, the more I become like Him—healthy, wise, and younger every day. I know I can't be perfect because He is still working on my ideal body (Philippians 3:21). When the trumpet sounds before the great tribulation on earth, He will give it to me. I will be so perfect that I will fly up to Him and meet Him in the clouds. No more whispers in my soul. Face to face.

I spent most of my life figuring out as a follower of Jesus whether I should be single, have a boyfriend, a girlfriend, a wife, and so on. I was exhausted, and I didn't get the answer until I rested and started chewing on Scripture day and night. While I was chewing on being like a tree replanted in Eden from Psalm 1:2–3, I imagined myself in Eden. Why Eden? Chewing is playing scenarios in my mind describing the goodness of God. I delete the analysis of good and evil. In Genesis, God took the first man out of Eden after he sinned. Now I am righteous in

Christ and replanted in Eden. In that garden, God created them, male and female. His presence has infused a solid masculine identity in my life. Now I see a woman, and just like Adam, I say, "Wow!" Note that lusting after a woman who is not my wife is not okay, so I quickly look the other way and see her as a sister. I meet with men, and I am now comfortable in my gender to be one of the guys without forcing myself to hunt, fish or watch football. I am naturally a man replanted in Eden and at ease with my gender identity and brand new heterosexual orientation. I enjoy the creative arts more than sports. These activities don't define my gender.

There's no effort, only the breath of my Redeemer as I chew His Word and renew my mind day and night. God promised Abraham a son while he was old and beyond the natural childbearing age. God instructed him to look at the ground during the day since his children would be as numerous as the dust. At night, he walked with His Maker and repainted each star as his own baby in his imagination. Why does Abraham need to replay the family dream in his mind day and night? Our fallen inner vision is programmed with negative expectations from birth because of Adam's fall. God cursed all of humanity because we are Adam's descendants. But He provided a way out to express His love alongside His justice. If we accept Jesus as our Savior, we become Abraham's spiritual children and inherit the same promises. The biological seed of Abraham is Israel. For some part of my journey, I did a morning devotion and slept after watching movies and the news. I was taking one step forward and one step backward, remaining where I was. The Scripture is clear on devotion and meditation—day *and* night. The turning point for me was to tune in to God's Word day and night.

After walking with Him in the cool of the garden, He had a new question for me: What can I do on earth to maximize my treasure in heaven? I don't want a tiny studio in heaven. I want a big mansion with many friends and significant responsibilities. I want to help Him run a perfect new world out of this world and soon entirely invade it. Rewards in heaven are essential. Without them, you will not be as happy as people who have them. And that degree of happiness will last forever.

I am an unlikely investor in stockpiling heavenly treasures since I am a man attracted to men. My first trades in the church caused me a lot of anxiety. Jesus is fighting all my battles, as I let not my heart be troubled with fear while I relax. Jesus is doing it for me and will do it for you. Yes, He is willing! Of course, the King of kings is able. He made the stars and the sun. You can stop reading and enjoy a mediocre life with a tiny studio in heaven.

Trust me, you will regret it forever. Heaven will be okay since you have barely made it from a fire with the smell of smoke while the rest of us who continue the journey will have a blast. So stay with me. If we never meet on earth, I will see you in heaven, and you will have many beautiful rewards, just like mine (John 14:2,

NKJV). The next chapters will help you schedule new activities on your earthly calendar to make it big in heaven.

CHAPTER 2

SPEAK THE HEAVENLY LANGUAGE

You will not go far if you can't speak the language when you travel to a new place. Every good gift comes from above. So how do you communicate in a heavenly language? How do you pray in tongues?

After accepting Christ (see Chapter 1), the Holy Spirit now lives in you. You become a candle that shines in the darkness. Not bad. Still mediocre. How about turning into a lamp powered by a never-ending flow of oil? The Holy Spirit will fuel you continuously. Ask God right now to baptize you in the Holy Spirit. He will never say no. He will never allow any other evil spirit to come in.

The Holy Spirit will put in your brain strange new words that you will not understand (Acts 2:4, TPT). He will not force you to say them. You are free to start and free to stop. It is a heavenly language that you don't understand and should be uttered in private or under your breath in public. It benefits only you. You are no longer praying selfish prayers since the Maker of heaven and earth is praying through you. When you say it, you rest in

Him. When you say it, power comes over you and activates talent, protection, and miracle-working energy.

Here is the first activity on your calendar. Speak in the heavenly language multiple times a day. It is effortless during a monotonous activity such as sitting in traffic. That will build you up, not with wisdom from me but with rivers of living water covering you from heaven. Wow! In the natural, it seems mundane and weird. Open your spiritual eyes, and the wonders will flow as your tongue moves to the Conductor's rhythm.

Put this book aside, and pray in tongues. Just say the words and let them out. Put your mind at rest. Engage your spirit fully.

On Mount Sinai, people disobeyed God and danced naked around the golden calf, engaging in all sorts of immorality. The Levites took their swords and killed many to execute justice out of divine righteous anger (Exodus 32:27, NKJV). Jesus had not died yet, and the Holy Spirit had not come to indwell the evangelicals of the day.

The Holy Spirit came rushing in like a mighty wind (Acts 2:2, TPT). He could not wait. The sword of the Spirit released many from their demonic bondage into salvation in Christ (Acts 4:31, TPT).

The upper room and Sinai are mirrors of my story and yours. God's justice cannot be bent, and His love is infinite. Jesus died to pay for our sins and show how deep

14

the Father's love is. His sacrifice pleased the Holy Spirit so much that He is rushing to be with you and speak through you. No prayer on earth is more vital than praying in tongues. You don't need to know the details. Kings look at the big picture and relax in their palace. You need to heal, use your gifts, get new talents, increase divine intervention, and stop the demonic influence.

Repeat after me. Hey Siri, Google Assistant. Schedule 15 minutes of praying in tongues every day. Do you want to declare your faith publicly? Find a local church, and get baptized in water. If you are in quarantine, get a bottle of water, pour it on your head, and send the video to your friends. Imagine me saying, "I baptize you in the name of the Father, the Son, and the Holy Spirit." It's a public declaration of faith that is needed just once. It is symbolized by water baptism. There is nothing magic in the water or in the hands of a pastor. All blessings come from above, from the pierced hands of Jesus. With a pandemic like COVID-19, what if you get sick? What if you have a preexisting condition? Does heaven have an Affordable Care Act?

CHAPTER 3

NO MORE SICK DAYS

You can't be sick on earth and invest in activities that give you a more massive treasure in heaven. You will need a robust and healthy body with no sick days. Yes, zero sick days from now on.

How? The answer is in your fridge and kitchen cabinets. Get water or fruit juice in a small cup. Get a tiny piece of bread or a cracker (Luke 22:7–8, TPT).

On a very unforgettable night, the night Jesus was betrayed by one of His disciples, Jesus took the bread and broke it. Take, He told us, this is my body broken for your healing. Eat the piece of bread in your hand (Matthew 26:26, TPT). See every stripe on the back of Jesus; there are hundreds of them. His bones were sticking out from the Jell-O of flesh and blood. Just like your teeth are crushing the bread, He was devastated. Take every mental and physical illness you have. You cannot possibly have more than hundreds. Each stripe can heal a disease. All you have to do is receive it. Don't focus on the symptoms. They will get worse. Focus on each stripe on His back. You will get healthier every day (Isaiah 53:5, NLT).

On the same night, Jesus held the cup. He said to drink it. Fruit juice, water, or wine—it does not matter. Drinking His blood does. Take a look at the cup you are holding in your hand. See every sin you have committed as a giant, ugly, dirty worm. Take another look, and see His blood dissolving every one of those giant, dirty worms. Nothing is left but pure wine. Now drink it. Receive His righteousness, so you will get what He deserves. Get all the blessings of healing, prosperity, and protection (Matthew 26:27–28, TPT).

Do this every day until Jesus calls you to come to Him. Put a reminder on your electronic calendar. Eat the body of Christ. Well done. Never raw. Jesus is the Lamb of God who takes away the sins of the world. Why did God instruct His people to take the Passover lamb fully roasted?

Elijah brought a sacrifice, and to demonstrate the power of God, He asked for a heavenly barbecue. Why not stars dancing or a thunderstorm with a musical composition? Nothing is random in Scripture. It is all about redemption—complete, full redemption (Luke 9:54, TPT).

Jesus, our sacrifice, after being beaten to a point where His body looked like a filet mignon, still cannot die and finish the work for us. God must kill God. Men cannot. Just like in Elijah's story, God sent judgment fire from heaven and roasted the body of Christ. The disciples first believed that the consuming fire of judgment should fall on the wicked. Still true. God is the same yesterday, today, and forever. If you traded places with the roasted Lamb, guess who gets roasted? Jesus. Guess who gets all the blessings that the Son of God deserves? You!

What's wrong with medium-rare? Sickness will not leave because it is impossible to separate the blood and the body. You don't separate body and blood when taking communion; you get sick and die. No other options. How can you separate? One answer. Barbecue. That is why matzo bread is pierced and has burned sections all over it. It represents the roasted body of Christ for healing that is paid for. God's fiery judgment fell on Christ instead of on you.

Sometimes God uses doctors to give us healing since we don't want them to go bankrupt. The principle does not change, but the method does. The stripes of Jesus provide the doctor wisdom to treat you. Also, Scripture mentions that the Word became flesh and dwelled among us. The Word, while reading it, also heals flesh, bones, and soul. It is described as a laser beam that pierces the marrow (Hebrews 4:12).

Now that you are healthy and guided by the Spirit, you are equipped to start your investment journey to stockpile heavenly treasures. If God's kingdom on earth is just like it is in heaven, can you benefit from these treasures sooner? What type of activities will the Holy Spirit lead you to do? Often, the devil hides as an angel of light. So it is essential to declare the nature of activities the Holy Spirit leads you to and not a detailed recipe.

There will be no formula. You have to listen directly to His instructions and have fun doing them. The rest of the chapters' goals are to help you discern His voice from the many evil voices that will crowd your spiritual trading floor. Once you have a revelation from Him, will your trust Him with a portion of your money?

CHAPTER 4

TITHE FOR A BOUNTIFUL HARVEST

Why should you support your local church with 10 percent of your income? It has enough money, and it is growing. You have bills that are multiplying.

God cursed talent, health, and opportunities that lead to financial benefits after Adam's fall. When you take out the tithe and dedicate it to God, you are asking God to replant you in the Garden of Eden before the fall. Your cup will overflow in a heavenly harvest because you have planted that financial seed. It is a money harvest. When you plant corn seeds, you will not get a tomato harvest. Plant money seeds, and watch God multiply them. Chapter 4 comes after Chapter 3. Tithing responds to the divine bread and the purifying wine (Genesis 14:18–20, NKJV). Dead people don't respond. Are you alive in Christ? The answer is in your bank statement. When you give God the tenth, He blesses the rest.

When should you start giving? When you receive a revelation from Jesus. There will be other voices that will compete with His. Where is the money going? What is the church doing with it? This money no longer belongs to you. God will guide the church to invest it wisely to spread the gospel. Is your church feeding you spiritually? Pay up just like you do at any store. Otherwise, the store will close. This is only a practical application. No angels are singing in the sky proclaiming the gospel. It is your job to do so through every open avenue by the Spirit.

God loves a cheerful giver. If you are cranky during the offering time for some reason or the other, giving will cause a dopamine rush in your brain and give you back priceless joy. When you take care of someone else and defocus on yourself, life begins. You can never outgive God. He will return so many blessings that your store-houses will be full—no one will be able to contain them anymore. Tithing is the root of pure wealth that does not fade away but multiplies to bless you and many people connected to you.

Now that you are healthy and wealthy, you have the tools to pursue your dream. These tools come from a divine redemption only possible through the sacrifice of Jesus. As you realize how much He loves you, His love will overflow to others so they want to help you get to the next level. Relational banking is as important as money.

There are three types of income globally: passive income, active income, and poverty income. Passive income seems excellent if you know what to invest in. It is subject to the cursed world and will fluctuate. Active income is a job that allows you to pay your bills as long as your health is okay and the market needs your services. Poverty income is a job that does not allow you to pay your bills. We all work. No one is unemployed in a practical sense. The benefits you get in these times are seeds you sowed in your government.

What about a divine income? It reverses the laws of the natural world after Adam's fall. If you give a tenth to your local church that preaches the gospel of grace, God will bless the 90 percent remaining. A seed must be sown in good ground in order to flourish. Suppose your church talks about social justice and the ten commandments and does not point people to a saving relationship in Christ. In that case, you are giving to a worldly social club. Make sure you sow in the excellent ground that proclaims the gospel of grace.

How is the rest blessed? You will have a spending budget for an active income and some fantastic ideas from the Spirit to a passive income. When Peter gave his boat to Jesus for a small amount of time to preach, Jesus did not give him back a prayer shawl. He overflowed his boat with fish to increase Peter's income as a fisherman. Before his tithe, Peter was cursed and struggling to make ends meet. Many wait to be financially stable. You tithe to become stable in your income flow.

God loves a cheerful giver and releases His trust in him or her. Giving brings you happiness as you overflow to others with blessings. Your church will have more resources to preach the gospel to the lost, and many more people will make it to heaven. There will be stockpiles of people in heaven. A real treasure. A place where Jesus is preparing not a small apartment but a mansion for you.

What about your talent? What is it? How can you add specific tasks on your calendar that turn into habits? Habits turn into great work that will bless many. All you have to do is open the gift from above (Chapter 5) and play it daily. Bury your talent, and it will be a huge problem when you meet the King of kings (Matthew 25:14–30, TPT). When you add value to your employer or customer through your talent, then your income will increase. You will have opposition to pursue your God-given talent. How can you overcome it?

CHAPTER 5

USE THE GIFT, ONE HABIT AT A TIME

God's gift can be useless if you don't use it. The dream is too big, and the tasks are overwhelming. His payment on the cross has given you all the supplies you need. So why do many fail? Striving and pushing closed doors will distract you from opening and using your gift. How do you find the open door?

So you compare yourself to others. You attack those who come against you—the naysayers. You give them your best argument only to have them tear you apart (Matthew 7:6). You worry all night about all the opportunities you have missed and everyone and everything that has come against you. You are way too worked up to notice. God's blessings are right there in your hands, right in front of you. Your emotional exhaustion is taking its toll; you are burning out. I have been there. .

The best way to chop at a large rock is one small piece at a time. If you have a five-year plan, it will paralyze you even more. One tiny activity that you enjoy is the start to break into an incredible future accomplishment that compounds with time. God has a big dream for you but listen carefully to His instructions. The first steps seem very small and insignificant. If you make a massive effort and don't finish, more discouragement will follow. Small steps over time become habits you no longer think about. Example: Thirty minutes of writing every day no matter what, one hour of welding, two hours of piano lessons, three hours of computer programming, and so on.

You have heard the typical advice—use your gift and talent—as if you don't know that already. If the devil has you locked up in your room, you cannot come to the Christmas tree and open the gift. The gift is the very desire of your heart. No one has to tell you to use it. The moment you see it, you will not be able to stop playing with it and thrive. The key is to get out of worry bondage and come out of your room of despair. Your gift is under the Christmas tree in the living room, but you are locked in your darkroom. The written Word of God is the way out.

Read the Scripture each day, and look for words that will jump at you and relate to your current circumstance. The devil can no longer lock you in a room of despair when you open your mouth and declare the written Word of God. He will flee! Then you can open the door after being locked in the room of depression and see the next steps you need to take at home with your spouse and children, at church, or at work. Jesus did not say it is preached by the rabbi. Jesus said it is written (Luke 4:4, TPT). When you are in a desperate place, your mind is under attack and will race faster than a preacher on your device. Your worry will drown the voice of the woman of God. When you read, you have to extract a divine comprehensive structure. When you remember what was written, your mental exit is at your own speed and will shift your mind from worry. When you speak what is written, your brain is now focused on your mouth instead of your circumstances. Your mind is receiving God's Word and goes into a calm and collected mode. The devil cannot devour you because God will not give you fear. The devil will run away. The Word dispatches angels to assist you. Every morning and every night, if you wash your brain with the Word, you will unlock the prison of despair. Then you can start a brand new day using your gift without mental restraints. You end your day with emotional healing after all the attacks you have endured during the day.

A widow was in debt and needed to take care of her family. A man of God asked her what was in her hand. Some oil and a jar. So she went door to door, asking for empty jars. She came back and started to fill them. She took the first steps, and God multiplied the oil. It never ran out until all the jars were filled. EVOO for sale. "Take some home today," she screamed in the marketplace (2 Kings 4:1–7, NLT).

She heard the gentle whisper of God that He wants her to prosper, and she confirmed the method with a man of God. She took the first steps. God multiplied her small resources. She went out to the market and not the local synagogue or government. Capitalism was born.

It is good to have emergency funds at churches or governments. Use them only if it is a clear indication from the Holy Spirit. There are no rules. Only flow with the rhythm of grace. Don't bury your talent and depend on others long-term. Wealth is created. When wealth is distributed, poverty comes on many. God does not like the spread of poverty, and He had a harsh punishment for the one who buried his talent (Matthew 25:14–30, TPT). Notice that the man who buried his treasure was afraid of his master. He did not believe that God was on his side. He was so worried and scared that he never unlocked his prison of despair with the good-news-from-Christ key. There was no record of him sinning to be thrown in outer darkness. Great misery and anguish intensify even more in that place. First, he got too attached to the demon of fear and did not believe God wanted to bless him. Although he came forward to accept the gift, he rejected the Giver by fear. Second, he did not use his talent. Fear is the cause of hiding your talent. Will I get paid for writing? Will I find a job if I submit my resume in this lousy economy? . Don't answer these questions now. Wash your brain with the Word continuously, and you will no longer ask them. You will step out, and nothing will stop you.

Once you have a lot of blessings and after you use your gifts, you can bless others. Remember, this is not your money, and God is not moved by need. You plant seeds on a need basis only, and you may be funding demonic operations. No harvest. Give where He wants you to give. People may look well dressed, all put together, hiding a big emergency. If you plant seeds in their life after you have peace from the Spirit, it will be multiplied in their lives and the lives of others.

There is another test of fear once you are rich. Are you trusting in God or your riches? It is not a question. It is a data point from your giving record (Luke 16:19–31, TPT). Salvation is by faith and not by works. But salvation works out because the light cannot be contained inside (Philippians 2:12–13, MSG). I picked out The Message translation on working out salvation in fear and trembling because it is not about typical fear and trembling. There are reverence and gratefulness to God. There are also so much energy and worship like excitement. It is essential not to fear and worry that God's blessings can flow to you because He knows you trust Him. In this context, fear is more like excitement on a roller coaster ride. It does not mean being scared that God is against you. Once you know that God is for you, the sky is the limit. It scares you a bit, but you can't wait to work out your salvation.

Notice that when Jesus speaks of hell, it is often a parable (fiction). Hell exists, and some will go there, but God will do everything kosher to reach out to people. His goal is that none should perish (2 Peter 3:9). But He will not force you to accept Jesus. He is a gentleman. How graceful God is! Chapter 5 represents the grace of God. Jesus asks us all to be His witnesses. But to whom? It will be a waste of time to preach to believers about salvation. They need to hear how to grow in grace. In these parables, Jesus gives us the marks of unbelievers so we can target them. Sometimes people become leaders in the church but don't have a personal relationship with the Lord. We looked at typical patterns to see when salvation is not working out in someone's life. Salvation is a superpower. If it is not working out, it does not exist yet.

That's how you make investments on earth to reap benefits here and in heaven. These investments are not working on the flesh, depending on visible needs. These habits are built by the flow of the Spirit. When you stand in front of Jesus, your work will not be in vain, and He will not burn it in flames. Yes! Yes! You will take it with you to heaven. Fill up the U-Haul. This all looks so smooth and easy—five graceful chapters—until the sixth intervention. Sodom and Gomorrah—a tale of two cities that can stop you dead in your tracks even if you are straight. Chapter 6 will be a bit scary. Six represents human effort without divine intervention. Reader, beware but fear not. Even with the threat of fire and brimstone, God wants what is best for you.

CHAPTER 6

THE NOW WORD: SODOM AND GOMORRAH

I am attracted to men while God leads me to read Sodom and Gomorrah's story and discover His loving heart. It sounds like a contradiction. Jesus closed the book on judgment and declared that from the time He stepped on earth until He comes back, it is the age of grace. It is the acceptable year of the Lord (Luke 4:18–21, TPT). God does not punish today. Only the devil attacks. We will learn from these two cities since all Scripture is kept for our instruction and growth in the faith. God is also a hero who defends the victims of crime. Let's dive in.

God hears the cry of injustice through innocent victims' blood (Genesis 18:20–21, MSG). The blood of humans speaks justice to its Maker. God has to be just. Today, the blood of Christ speaks a better Word.

God was counting with Abraham the number of righteous people in Sodom. Is that just like a random exercise? Or did Abraham forget that his cousin is one person? How did Abraham become righteous? By faith. His works were terrible. He lied, he gave his wife to a harem, and he slept with the maid. After the grain, wine (communion), and tithing, he is ready to evangelize righteousness by faith. Abraham did not remain the same but became better and better every day. Lot, who is living in Sodom, got it and became righteous. But he did not preach grace; he was preaching the law.

Even after years of being disciplined by Abraham on the gospel of grace and justification by faith alone, Lot switched to law preaching. Abraham saw the star constellations from Virgo (virgin birth of Jesus) to the Cross constellation where justice is served to Leo (the Lion of Judah returns). Our flesh will move naturally under the law when injustice occurs. It takes flowing with the Spirit to be able to swim upstream. The Spirit rushes to you like a mighty wind when you focus on the death and resurrection of Jesus. He loves it!

This is a dangerous place. It is a natural reaction, but the desired holiness cannot be sustained. You ask people to do good for adequate treatment from God, but the law cannot lift a finger to help them. Grace is not lawless. Jesus completes the law. With the power of no condemnation, the righteous can go and sin no more. A man cannot cheat on his wife under the law, but he may still want to, especially in moments of conflict or distance. Under grace, a man goes above and beyond the law's expectation and treats his wife like a queen because the same Spirit that raised Jesus from death lives in him. There is a divine power that enables him to accomplish amazing things for his family. He abides by the commandments and exceeds expectations because he is no longer doing it through self-effort but through Christ, who gives him strength. Husbands are faithful to their wives to the point of death, just like Jesus and His church.

God's law is stringent. If you violate one clause, no matter how tiny it is, you are guilty of it all. Being under grace takes practice. .Under grace, the consuming fire of God falls on Jesus, and He takes our place. The desire for justice is natural. Some punish themselves, and some go out of their way to punish others. Be like that one disciple, John, who came to the cross and looked up. He needed no extra explanation and no extra strength. The rest ran away in despair at that moment.

Mr. Lot learned the lesson of grace but switched to a hazardous "Do Not" under pressure. Most people are like Lot; they rely on common sense and don't practice grace. The corruption under the law intensifies to an uncontrollable state. Only grace can stop it. The goodness of God can eliminate the evil desire of humans so they become holy by accident. That way, Jesus gets 100 percent of the glory. You wake up, and your addiction is gone—nowhere to be found—if you stop trying to change and start delegating addictive habits to Dr. Jesus. Addictions are addictive, and only the Son can set you free.

Lot said, "Please, my brothers, do not do something so wicked" (Genesis 19:7, AMP). What is the heart of Je-

sus for Sodom (Matthew 11:23)? If that city experienced
unmerited miracles, it would have remained until today.
This is very strong! Israel is the only nation remaining
from that time. God would have spared Sodom if they
had the right preacher. It is essential to pick the right local
church with guidance from the Spirit in a place that feeds
you and doesn't beat you.

The preached law made the men's sins greater. First,
they asked to engage in intimate encounters with Lot's
visitors. New flesh in town, it seemed. Their addiction
was so intense that the men who lived there could not
meet it anymore. After Lot preached the law to stop them,
they became more violent. God is just, and he destroyed
Sodom. God and Abraham were counting the righteous
earlier. God cannot pour judgment on the city if fifty
remain there. Lot left. What about the rest? They went
to a better place called Zoar and stayed there. Although
Scripture does not spell it out, I believe that God and
Abraham were counting on the righteous to go live in a
city of refuge and thrive. There were more than fifty who
left Sodom and were saved for two reasons. God is the
same yesterday, today, and forever. Just like Jesus wants
to spare as many in Sodom as possible, so does God.
There is no better explanation for God and Abraham to
count for people outside of Lot's direct family since they
know how many already are in Lot's family.

The angels told Lot to take refuge in Zoar, a small
town close to Sodom that was not destroyed. Lot, in

despair, left to the mountains. He was afraid of getting known there, but that was a place of refuge, and his fear, driven by a bent toward the law, drove him out from an ideology of blessings yet again. He heard the angel of the Lord but did not trust him. He was still attached to what he saw in the natural and what the law considers good or evil. What is the importance of a city of refuge like Zoar? Jesus declared this on the cross: forgive them, Father, for they don't know what they are doing. According to Moses's law, a city of refuge is for people who commit crimes by mistake. Jesus became our city of refuge. That's why it was so crucial for Lot to leave Sodom and go to Zoar. He did not listen and gave birth to an evil nation—the Moabites—out of his own daughters after getting drunk. It gets ugly very quickly when you don't head toward your city of refuge—Jesus on the cross—and live there.

Happiness is when you know that you pleased your Daddy God and when you enjoy each moment, casting all your cares about tomorrow on Him. He is our refuge (Psalm 62:8). If you feel dirty, there is a fountain filled with blood to cleanse your guilty stains. Smelly people need a bath. Come dirty, and plunge beneath the flood of His blood and get cleansed. Come boldly to the throne of grace. Have fun hanging out with Jesus! The veil between you has been broken. The more you fill up on His love, the more your friends want to invite you to experience the overflow of His love in you. The moment you come guilty is the moment you feel depressed. But the Father will ignore your pity party and throw you a party worthy of a son after the fatted calf has been killed (Luke 15:11–31, TPT). The lawful brother rejected the invitation; he depended on his merit. The show will go on without him. Who wants grumpy around anyway? Notice that the Passion Translation changed the title. I love it! It is no longer about the Prodigal Son, and the focal point matches the title now—The Loving Father. Let's dance! Jesus is in the house.

CHAPTER 7

RELAX AND ENJOY SOME ENTERTAINMENT - PARTY WITH THE FATHER!

Mortgage. Projects at work. Kids. Grandpa fell and broke his hip. Pandemics and economy. Party? Really? Even if you go, you will not enjoy it. You are camping in the valley of the shadow of death. You fear all possible evil. You think a spa day or a weekend getaway may be a good idea.

Your body gets away among green pastures and still waters. Your brain is in a prison of hopelessness. It will keep spinning on the bicycle of despair. No matter how exotic your escapade, you come back more tired than when you started. The relaxing environment wears off very quickly if your head is doing laps on the worry track. You try yoga and meditation to force yourself to relax. It gets worse. Where is God?

He is completely exhausted and spent. Every joint of His body has been pulled apart (Psalm 22:14, TPT). God is dead. His spiritual seed will fill the earth with the glorious good news—it is finished! Your rest is only found in His calvary. Look no further. His pierced hands deliver the only true shalom you need.

At His palace, what will we lack? Nothing (Psalm 23:1, TPT). And even we will have more than what we need. How long will we dwell there? Forever (Psalm 23:6, NKJV).

Let's step out into His backyard. A big sign hangs before you. See the beautiful landscape? Carve your heart in the shape of these letters: I always have more than enough. The harmony in nature will then resonate with the peace inside you.

Then step into green pastures and still waters. Body, mind, and soul restoration on the way. Step by step, round and round you go to get to the top of the hill of glory. Each step you take follows His footsteps of righteousness. Don't follow self-help advice. Don't follow your plan to get back on track. Follow the pierced feet that paid for all your luxury living on earth as well as in heaven.

The aromatherapy of the anointing oil that reveals the fragrance of the Holy Spirit will crown your head and enlighten your smells. You don't need to cook or use any self-effort. He prepared a table for you with overflowing goodness to confront every enemy. Mortgage: paid.

Projects at work: completed with excellence. Kids: smiling and behaving. Grandpa's heath: better than a young stallion. Take one-fourth cup of Dead Sea salt, and add it to a hot bath—light a rosemary mint candle to bring in the smells of Jerusalem. Get a poster of green pastures in your bathroom. Enjoy a glass of virgin champagne: Perrier. Soak in the goodness and mercy that will hunt you down for the rest of your life—an unending spa day.

Now that you are chill and come out smelling like Jesus, you will become the life of the party. Grumpy was buried under the Dead Sea bath. Nonbelievers would love to come and visit to see what they are missing.

Remember, we are not the head of Christ. We are the body of Christ. So many people hurt out there—sheep without the Shepherd. Not you. The Lord is your Shepherd—you shall not want. He fills you up so you can overflow with blessings to others.

Some need a smile. Others need a hug. Some need someone to be present with a body leaning forward to signal care. You are the body of Christ, so use your body language. Leave room for the head of the church (Jesus) to speak to their heart. God gives you rest. Share it with your brothers until God gives them the same rest He gave you (Joshua 1:12–15, MSG).

Many will be just like you—overflowing with joy. Celebrate with them, and have fun! The needy will drain you while the merry hearts will fill you back up. That secret time with Jesus in still waters will restore your soul. Rinse daily.

On the third day, there will be an extravagant wedding (John 2:1, TPT). Be there in your best suit. People will run out of wine and intoxicating joy. You will not. Fill their jars from the rivers of living water that come out of you, and teach them to get that living water from Jesus. It will not stay just water. He will turn it into a joyful celebration. Why on the third day? No real, lasting joy can come without the cross and the resurrection—no wine without crushing grapes.

Demonic thieves will make their way into the temple to make the house of God a den of thieves. You cannot enjoy a peaceful celebration with them in that place. You have to burn those bridges and turn the tables like Jesus did (John 2:13–17). One avenue is to cast out the demons that live in people's bodies using your authority as a believer. Some people enjoy the company of demons; you have to put boundaries between you and them at this point. Check your invitation list, and don't be afraid with guidance from the Spirit to uninvite and unfriend. Then the joy of your house party will be reaching its full potential.

When you get out in the world, whether to get entertained or to work, take the table with you. Your enemies come at you. You have a table of plenty in a world of lack. Savor each bite calmly, knowing His goodness and mercy will confront and win against evil from others and your own mistakes.

Life is now abundant. Chilling comes naturally as you are well taken care of, and you can party with friends and family in the presence of Jesus with no care in the world. He took care of your lack at the cross. All paid for. What do you do when, during that peace, enemies start to throw fiery darts at you? Sure, He took care of the lack. What about the attack?

CHAPTER 8

WIN THE WAR WITH THE PROPHECIES SPOKEN OVER YOU

Samuel did not shy away from fighting bravely for justice (1 Samuel 15:33, AMP). The righteous anger of Samuel the prophet could not be contained. The voice of God is clear and precise. Agag, the king of the Amalekites, became a good friend of Saul, king of Israel. Association with evil displeases God. Agag has used his sword and the power of his reign to make many women childless. Many children were aborted under his dominion. He deserved the death penalty.

Does God want us today to be engaged in a just war to end injustice? Not yet. We will be soldiers fighting with Jesus after the tribulation. Today, our role is to preach the gospel, cast out the demons that cause people to commit evil without their will, and heal the sick. Our warfare is not against flesh and blood yet but against the principalities of evil. But grace has a period. People will not become better with their own efforts but will be changed by grace. Grace does not let injustice go on forever. Its period is an expression of love for all the victims of evil. Jesus is grace.

Saul consulted with everyone—the people, the prophet, and even the enemy's king. Samuel met with him so many times, and in the end, the teacher was sick of teaching and left. After killing Agag, Samuel never saw Saul again. Saul received from God through Samuel (1 Samuel 15:1, AMP) and failed.

David received from God directly after asking the Maker of heaven and earth whether he should attack the Amalekites (1 Samuel 30:8, AMP). What? His wives and family were raped and captured. The Amalekites did much damage unprovoked. His men wanted to stone him because he stood there and did nothing. Wasn't it obvious based on the common law of a just war that God would say yes? David finds strength in his invisible companion and follows His voice. So should you so you can succeed. There is no formula, only a relationship with Him. You call on Jesus first. Put down that phone when you are in trouble. First, go to the King of kings for advice. He may lead you to an advisor as a resource, but He is the only source. The next step may involve a social alliance arranged by the Lord, and it may not. Follow Him.

An Egyptian employee was fired after getting sick and being declared useless. David's men fed him (notice bread and raisins, shadows of Christ's body and blood for healing). God used the One the world rejects for His glory. He could have used a star to lead David to the Amalekite. I love how egraceful our Daddy is. He led David to the enemy camp and gave honor to workers treated unjustly, fired after being sick (1 Samuel 30:13, AMP). God had to lead David to release a complete stranger first. It sounds counterintuitive. His wives were captive, and the clock was ticking. David should focus on himself and his needs first. This is where people get depressed and never win. Help others first, and see how God will help you. Why?

Because when you live in luxury, you don't mind stopping and smelling the roses or volunteering at a soup kitchen. When you are in trouble, trouble consumes you. Snap out of it! You are a child of the highest God. You walk through a dark, dangerous alley, yes. Keep walking to the Light. Don't sit on a rocking chair in the shadow of death complaining, "I will never get out of this challenging situation." When you help others, you are no longer focusing on your own misery. It is one step closer to your own happiness. Assisting others forces you to let go of your own worry. When you let go, God has room to work on your problem and fix it.

Then David fought the battle against the Amalekites and won. He freed his family from captivity. Who gets paid for fighting? Wait. People who did not fight made the same money (1 Samuel 30:24). Yet David shined as the man after God's own heart. He knew the battle belonged to the Lord, and God did all the real fighting and brought the enemies into their hands. Never once did David consult with the prophet Samuel. He had a direct line to God, and so should you. Saul relied on everyone from prophets to witches and never on the Lord. Samuel the prophet anointed both Saul and David. Saul used the prophet. David used the prophecies spoken over him. What was above David?

A horn is made from a dead ram (a sacrifice pointing to Jesus). That horn was filled with anointing oil. The drumbeat of the gospel never ceases. Samuel positioned the horn above David's head, and David received it. The cornucopia symbolizes the prophecy spoken over him. He did the same for Saul, but Saul did not receive it. Thousands of years later, Paul asked Timothy, his disciple, to fight the spiritual war. Today, we fight evil spirits in the invisible realm by casting them out, using our authority from Jesus. We are spiritual warriors in the age of the acceptable year of the Lord. After we come back to earth from heaven with Jesus, we will become physical warriors to end evil on the ground in the days of God's judgment. Paul asked Timothy to fight the spiritual war with the prophecies spoken over him (1 Timothy 1:18–19, TPT).

Paul tells Timothy to use prophecies as weapons as he rages spiritual warfare right in the first chapter. It is sandwiched by two primary sections—a moral strategy and then a moral compass.

A moral strategy should not include digressions on

genealogies and distractions with tradition. It causes people to debate all day with no fruit. Grace's apostle is not rejecting the law, but he uses it as a tool for the right job. In a court of law, the law is needed. He cites some examples: rapists, liars, homosexual offenders, and so on. The Aramaic translation of homosexual offenders points to rape. It reflects the story of Sodom where men wanted to break into a house to force intimacy with some men in it.

Some dive into Leviticus right after restrictions on men sleeping with women in their menstrual period. Intercourse of men with men has the same nature as it causes fractures in tissues that invite more infections than usual. Abomination correctly translated means, in that context, disgusting at the sight of blood and high disease risk. We should not take these passages out of their context and condemn people who struggle, especially at puberty, to figure out their sexuality. They will feel terrible about themselves, and it will arrest their self-esteem. It may also cause them to harm themselves. The word of our loving Father always builds up—it never tears people apart. What are the three tools that God uses to build us up?

There is a medical fact in Leviticus 18 about tissue fracturing when two men have an intimate relationship. This is not an excuse to become an accuser of our brothers. This is the devil's job. But tissue fracturing is unhealthy. It causes a complete shutdown of the immune system after a high number of attempts. That means diseases of all sorts will manifest in a way that will make the human body experience extreme pain and be covered with sores to the point of death. This process may be delayed with modern medicine but not canceled.

Jesus on the cross delivered us from the extra divine punishment since He took it all on His body. He did not rescue us from the consequences of sin. If I put my finger in a fire, it will burn, but God will not beat me up for it. He already punished Jesus. As I grow up in Christ, no one needs to tell me not to run into the fireplace. I have some good Christian friends I love and respect who decided to stay in a same-sex relationship without engaging in intercourse. A romantic relationship without intimacy ceases to be romantic. We are called to flee from sexual immorality and not get close enough. I respectfully disagree and don't feel peace from the Spirit or confirmation from the Word about it.

Sexual passion has a consuming spiritual nature that brings two flesh into one and cannot be treated as a remote-controlled video game. Staying next to someone I am attracted to in bed every night and not thoroughly exploring my passion is impossible for me. So I personally run like Joseph did. .

Lesbian relationships don't affect the immune system. Women in those relationships don't have a gender identity assurance like Eve before the fall. Some want to make a small change in clothing, and some pursue surgery. The surgeon and psychiatrist provide acceptance but do not guarantee stability in a gender role after treatment. There is no condemnation here for people who choose to stay in a lesbian union. Abundant life in Christ includes getting replanted in the Garden of Eden. These consequences lead me to conclude that same-sex romantic relationships in all forms and formats are not in God's original design. They are derived from the fall. A loving Daddy God will lead us out of it as we have a daily assurance of our gender role infused by His breath in Eden. He will build us up with three tools—no condemnation, healthy habits for our body, and gender identity assurance. No condemnation in Christ takes people to heaven in the future. Healthy habits and emotional ease bring heaven on earth here and now. We covered so far a moral strategy that we can work on perfecting in our quiet study. It will feed our brain food to be able to function later. In the heat of the battle, we need a moral compass.

Remember, we have to listen directly to God, and there is no formula. We are not followers of Jesus under the law but under grace. Does that mean you do what you want? Yes, if God sanctifies what we wish. A demonic spirit impersonates us and makes us think that an unhealthy habit is what we want. That demon is very skilled at mimicking our inner voice. We are, in fact, doing what that demon wants, thinking this is what we want. This is not our true self, but we may be tricked into believing it is. The more we contemplate and chew on Scripture, the more we can discern the voice of the Lover of our soul, Jesus. When He fulfills our heart's desires, these desires are never unhealthy since they come from a loving and wise Daddy God. It is not okay to sin. Christ completes the law by granting us desires to win. The demons that tricked us all these years run away to the pigs, never to return again.

After years of burgers and root beers, I have a large belly. So I started going to the gym. I looked at my gut on the first day. Still big. Second day. Same. The third day…I could go on, but you get the point. Muscles come by exercising and exercising, and exercising…faith comes by hearing and hearing and hearing. I can't join the army when I'm overweight and huff and puff when I run. I must be fit. It's the same with spiritual warfare. There must be a build-up of faith by hearing the Word of Christ over a long period.

So why do people lose the battle? They hear the law that is holy and just but cannot grant power to win over sin. They feed on "Do Nots." They end up fat with an evil that increases and gives them more trouble. The strategic morality belongs in a courtroom to convict criminals like the rapists Paul talks about. It has its place. The judge has a long time to examine the evidence and read 600 pages of laws. To win spiritual warfare, you need prophecies and a moral compass to quickly point you where to make the right move in a swift battle.

Prophecies are a collection of good news for you. You will be crowned with a helmet of salvation, so to speak, to fight. Salvation is not just deliverance from hell, but it is abundant life here and now, no matter what mistakes you make. You have to hear that good news again and again to develop a fighting faith. Just like the gym, it takes time to get a six-pack if you have a large belly. Half an hour on Sunday is not enough. Daily training is required with messages on the death and resurrection of Christ. Paul was so angry in some of his letters when people discussed circumcision. I feel like he was banging on the table and saying, "I want nothing preached among you except Jesus and Him crucified!"

The shepherds saw a bright light on Christmas night. They were trained under the law, and they were told they can never become rabbis, just the lowest of the lows. So when they saw the divine light, they freaked out. Just like God did on Mount Sinai after giving the law, they were scared that they would get the justice they deserved. It was a great surprise to hear goodwill and peace to mankind. A lamb is sitting in a manger that will be the Lamb of God who takes away all their sins! Forever forgiven! Nothing they do can upset God since His Son took their place to receive all the judgment. They know how lambs and priests work. The righteousness of the good Lamb is now transferred to the sinner. This is not your typical Lamb! This is God Himself getting slain so they will enjoy unmerited intimacy with God. That's why these shepherds ran to the baby Jesus. You can reread hundreds of verses that hide the secrets of redemption and extract it. This is how you will develop a solid helmet of salvation. Shepherds, prostitutes, and tax collectors who cheat their own people quickly understood the message of Jesus. They were at the end of their ropes. Disciples and Bible scholars took them a long time.

This will now be your moral compass. You don't have time when the devil attacks to read 635 laws. That's for a judge in a court of law, not for a warrior. Your moral compass says this automatically: forever forgiven, all sins past, present, and future. That truth and grace are so ingrained in you that it is like brushing your teeth. It just happens by itself. Against that, what can the devil, the accuser of the brethren, accuse you of? When his accusations fall to the ground, your shame evaporates. With no condemnation, shame, and guilt, you are empowered to go and sin no more. Does that mean you ignore the moral strategy and stop studying the ideas that are coming from God? No. One is food in your quiet time (moral strategy), and the other one is like two legs to run in the right direction (moral compass). You need the food to be able to run and not faint.

What other prophecies can you use at war? When you pray in tongues, it is also a new covenant prophecy, and it is quick and fit for battle. You utter the words the Spirit puts in your head, and bam! Rivers of living water will shield you in a 360-degree waterfall around you, quenching all the fiery darts of demons. The moment you feel uncomfortable, this habit will kick in. Why? Because in Chapter 2, we scheduled a daily tongue prayer on your calendar. So now it is a habit.

The Shepherd Jesus will speak to His sheep, and they will hear His voice. Other voices are evil. As your faith develops, your signal-to-noise ratio will improve. That is your moral compass when making a decision on the next step. It is not a strategy for a five-year plan. It is daily bread only. In the beginning, you will make the wrong decisions by hearing the wrong voices and mistake them for Jesus. It is okay—He will use it for your good, and your signal from Him to noise from the enemy ratio will get better. That's how Paul ends the first chapter on a moral compass and how some people lose it and suffer as a consequence.

Winning the spiritual war is just amazing! With all due respect, it is better than a miracle. When we go where God does not lead, we can get seriously hurt and waste time and resources. Nothing we do can affect the strong salvation by the blood. But the anxiety period waiting for the miracle to arrive is not an indication of abundant life. Some miraculous acts manifest 100 percent, some thirty-fold, then sixty, then 100. Go ahead and develop a good moral compass to win the battles at a high frequency. It is essential to distinguish an ethical strategy for a just society from a moral compass for personal growth.

Jesus will never lead you to unhealthy habits, and you don't have to analyze a penal code at all. Why? He is super smart, will not make mistakes ever, and loves you. You only follow His prompting. When you examine a code in a battle, sin will increase, and you will lose and surrender. Under grace, the moral compass does not make you think about good and evil. It is a walk with Jesus yoked to His movement. It is honest and even goes above and beyond law and order. You don't want to steal. No one you know can give to the work of the gospel more than you do. You are not going to let it happen. You don't want to cheat, but instead you love from all your heart. There is no 700-page instruction manual to do that. Just follow Jesus.

Caleb followed God and His prophecies and promises. God promised them the land, and no giant can negate that. As a result, Caleb got younger every day, fought giants, and made it to the Promised Land. Many were afraid of the giants. He knew God was bigger and lived as if he knew against all cultural influence and massive demonic attacks. He lived his own truth and dared to be different. Caleb did not have a different skin color or personality type. Still, he had a purpose and steps guided from above. Caleb could have been tricked by the Torah into not testing God by exposing himself to danger. The giants were sure dangerous, but Caleb followed the Word specifically tailor-made for him. All the people used only the data they could see and forgot about the power of the One who parted the Red Sea for them. Caleb looked at the prophecies over his head and not the voice of the majority around him. Eight out of ten members of his committee voted against fighting the giants.

Caleb won the spiritual war and was young, at eighty-five, and very successful. He fought with prophecies. You will be successful as well, my dear reader, in the mighty name of Jesus. Should you continue on this journey all alone? Loneliness hurts even in Paradise and even after winning many spiritual wars.

CHAPTER 9

BIG DO NOT: IT IS NOT ACCEPTABLE TO STAY ALONE

Jesus revealed Himself as Messiah to a woman with one side trick and many husbands. You are amazing! Keep telling those self-righteous conservatives that they are a collection of evil snakes. Every tongue that rises against you, you will condemn. This is your inheritance as righteous in Christ. #ownit.

Why should you stand up for yourself? Because the pastor's anointing flows over his congregation. When a prophet anoints with oil, the oil drips on the beard and the body. Both right and false prophecies are above your head. Move under an umbrella that protects you.

The Messiah invites you to sit under the umbrella of grace.

Where the rain of sin falls heavy, grace gets stronger and deflects every drop.

It is not suitable for a man to be alone (Genesis 2:18,

AMP). In the original Hebrew, it reads like a balancing act. Men and women complement each other. So God created a life partner for Adam with whom he had romantic intimacy. Adam was walking with God, and that happened before the fall. How can we reconcile that to the Apostle Paul calling people to remain single if they can? It is better than getting married, he claimed (1 Corinthians 7:7, TPT). Are they out of balance? God is the same yesterday, today, and forever. Only our perception of the matter needs digging in Scripture and guidance from the Holy Spirit. Unless someone has no power over passions, then marriage is better than a battle with lust. It is getting trickier. What if those passions are of a same-sex nature?

Is having a boyfriend part of God's will for a man? Romans 1 does not only include same-sex orgies but also includes leaving the natural order of heterosexual relationships. This is key for an abundant sexual orientation and gender identity restoration in the Garden of Eden. Whether single or married, a man who is comfortable in his gender identity will experience happiness and fulfillment. A single man will be blessed and will have more time for the Lord and His ministry. A married man and his wife will mirror Christ and the church. The devil does his best to distort that image. "Not today. Not Now. Not ever again" (Hillsong music).

Same-sex loving relationships can provide a short-term atonement of gender identity fluidity. I do not condone those, and I love everyone who makes that choice

without any conditions. But this gender lack of ease is
not God's will. God has an abundant life for all of us and
wants to replant us in the Garden of Eden and restore our
masculine or feminine identity. It is part of the benefits
package when we seek first His righteousness. We may
not use it immediately, or the devil may put a veil on our
eyes for us to be blinded to it. But it takes incredible people in our lives to ask us great questions. That is why it
is essential to remain open in community and get insight
from the Holy Spirit, confirmed in the Word and other
mature believers. Maturity does not depend on age but on
exposure to the Word.

In a community with others, there is a risk of con-
tracting various diseases. Jewish tradition had a big "Do
Not." Do not eat without washing your hands. Jesus
cooked a big dinner for his disciples, and no one, including Him, washed their hands.He wanted to emphasize
that the negative words that come out of your mouth will
pollute you. Negative words cause people to be divided
and isolated. Words have nutritional value for your soul
and emotions. If you meditate on the grace of Jesus day
and night, uplifting stories will come out of your mouth.
If you watch violent and sexually charged movies, you
will transmit what you receive.

I was serving the homeless community in my city.
Their hygiene was a little over the top, so the Holy Spirit
led me to use hand sanitizer for my team and me. I could
have opened my Bible, analyzed 200 verses, and come up

with a conclusion—maybe or maybe not. This is where, in a practical situation, the moral strategy will never work. You have little time to act and do it right. I needed a functional moral compass.

Later on, the moral strategy works well. In a community with a massive attack from demons of infirmities, the human immune system needs some help to survive. Hand sanitizers are perfect. Why not miracles? There are two reasons: develop a loving relationship with Jesus, and follow his sweet aroma and enjoy life. The second reason is that miracles alone make doctors and pharmacies bankrupt. God created their brains and raw ingredients to help us. A moral strategy is excellent for training purposes and awakens in you the need for a Savior. It does not save you.

As a single man, I have more time for Jesus, and He is equipping me to fight the battle against lust and to win on autopilot without struggles. This is not advice on relationships for my readers. Why? Jesus showed me that next step. He may show you something completely different. There is no formula—only a relationship with Him. I am a perfect friend with all my exes, but I am a terrible lover. I cannot give advice on something I am weak at. I boast in my weakness because that is where God's grace operates at its best. Will I remain single? I no longer think about it. It is a day-by-day and date-by-date guidance. If someone comes along and I feel peace from the Spirit, then I will get hitched.

There is an excellent counselor, an incredible Savior, and His name is Jesus. Talk to Him about what the next step is for you today. He will give you your daily bread and not overwhelm you with a five-year plan. What friends to go with for dinner? Go on a second date or not? And so on. Jesus will show you a concrete next step. Sometimes the next step is to go talk to a wise human counselor whom you trust. But don't go until you have peace from the Spirit.

You want to appoint a deacon. The leader's life at home, if it is stable, is an excellent point for his background check. Like the Apostle Paul states in Corinthians, a single man can be a tremendous leader with a new divine ability to control lust. Jesus said, "I am the way, the truth, and the life" (John 14:6, NKJV). Who asked Jesus for grace in any area, including sex, and Jesus refused?

No one! All who came to Him were made whole. When he saw a demoniac, did He send him more insults and tell him he was an abomination? He healed him. After He healed him, He instructed him to preach the gospel of compassion (Mark 5:18–20, TPT). He did not preach in one city, in two cities, in three cities, but in ten cities (Decapolis). He put a lot of miles on His sandals. How do we treat the outcasts in our community? Do we reach out like Jesus did with that demoniac to transform His life?

In his book *What's So Amazing about Grace?* Philip Yancey records a conversation with a man and his mother. The man said, "As a gay man, I've found it's easier for me to get sex on the streets than to get a hug in church." His mother answered in a sweet, quavering voice, "He may be an abomination, but he's still our pride and joy."[1]

We all fall short of the glory of God. He loves us so much, and we are his pride and joy. He died on the cross to rescue us. Not all churches and believers are uncomfortable with same-sex attractions. It is possible to be planted in the house of the Lord and connect with fellow believers.

I wanted to share my struggle with a trusted friend. He is a well-respected minister with a beautiful wife and kids. He preached to hundreds and pointed many to Jesus, and they all were healed. He used to pick me up to go swimming. That day I decided we would take two cars. For me, I felt like it was the end of the world or my world as I know it. I did not want to be left stranded, so I took my own car, and he took his. I spilled my beans, and he did not even care. He continued speaking like nothing had happened. We continued hanging out at the lake and talked about boats. So weird. I thought he was just pleasant to my face and that we would never speak again. Then he uttered some words that changed my life:

"Let's go get pizza!"

Those very words came alive to me. The body of

---

1 Philip Yancey, *What's So Amazing about Grace?* (Grand Rapids, MI: Zondervan, 1997), 66.

Christ was the body of Christ. No artificial ingredients were added. This was my point of no condemnation. I have the power to go and sin no more, to become all that God created me to be. We had a fantastic dinner, and I have never felt love like that in my entire life. Christ is the head. The church is the body. Sometimes we really need to be seen, heard, and touched. We need the body of Christ. My friend never asked me about my private life at all. He did something absolutely insane, or I thought. He asked me to preach the gospel with him to people on the streets.

I went to a 7-Eleven to get a homeless lady some chicken wings. I came back, and the gentle voice of Jesus inside me told me to ask her if she wanted to accept Jesus. She said yes! I memorized the salvation prayer from Pastor Joel Osteen on TV the night before. I spit it out quickly, fearing that something terrible would happen to me. She got saved. I prayed for another one, and she got healed and no longer had to use her wheelchair.

I got into the groove, and I got addicted to preaching the gospel. But wait! My resume does not qualify me. Jesus asked me to look at His resume and put my name on top. Can I do this? Am I qualified? I hear the Apostle Paul banging this on the table: I want to hear nothing among you except Jesus and Him crucified! His qualification and grace operate at a high level in the middle of my weakness.

What a Savior! He saw the woman at the well. He asks her for a favor. Five husbands and one trick on the side did not add a lot of moral value to her spiritual account. Maybe it's finding the right mountain to worship on, or is it Jerusalem? What? She, the immoral woman, knew He is the Messiah first. What? No accountability? No questions on remaining sober for at least 24 months before qualifying for a ministry calling (John 4:1–30, TPT)? What? I experienced her moment...

A drop-in-the-bucket moment!

Run and preach the gospel—no need to draw water from the well of this world. Jesus has done it for the Samaritan woman with six lovers, for millions of believers who depend only on Him and for me. He can do it for you. Accept the challenge to share the good news.

CHAPTER 10

FILL UP ALONE TO DRIVE FARTHER TOGETHER

Decapolis! Ten cities!

The demoniac had a mob of demons. Jesus delivered him to deliver the good news to ten cities! So will you. He needed sandals, rested feet, and a quiet time to recharge. You need shoes, gas for your car, and a filled-up soul.

Be still in His presence.

Ask Him to mute your notifications. Some come from devices, some come from humans, and the rest come from your worried brain. Driven by a passion for his people's suffering, Moses could not bury an Egyptian, and he was quickly busted. When he stood still, an entire army of Egyptians drowned in the Red Sea. The good news of the gospel today drives demons out and saves souls. Our battle is not against flesh and blood, and trusting God quietly remains the only way to win. Stand still to fill up. You can't put gas in your car while driving. You have to park and turn the engine off.

Way before the sun rose, the Son rose. He prayed alone. Late in the day, his friends could not find him (Mark 1:35–37). People were asking for him when they woke up. So He must have spent hours with the Father. He did not want any interruptions, so He made sure His friends could not bother Him.

Jesus is a member of the Trinity and has no sin. He has been talking to God from the past forever to the future outside time. Why time alone and away from humans? He is part human now. Although sinless, He is surrounded by human sins. The Scripture does not reveal the conversation or lack thereof.

In other situations, the conversation between the Father and the Son is revealed. In His baptism, God told Jesus, "You are My beloved Son, in whom I am well pleased" (Mark 1:11, NKJV). At the cross, Jesus cried, "*Eli, Eli. lama azavtani?*" (Psalm 22:1, OJB)—"My God, my God,…Why are you so far from helping Me, and from the words of my groaning?" (Psalm 22:1, NKJV). The original language keeps the sound of lamentations.

The conversation goes from encouragement coming from above to crying out to God from below. Sometimes there is complete silence. His presence cleans out the dust of sin that the world has deposited on the righteous in Christ. As Jesus is, so are we in this world. If He needs uninterrupted time with the Father, we sure do. It should never be legalistic but a longing of your heart. Nobody has to convince me to stop at Buc-ee's when I'm on a road trip in Texas. I love that place! This is exactly how I spend my time alone with God. First, I really want to, and of course, I need to. Jesus gives you good desires and removes the evil desires. Just relax, numb yourself, and let Him operate on your heart.

Lashes after lashes striped His back. At the cross, God refused to hear the cry of Jesus! Previously, with every quiet time together, God was very close to His Son. The soldiers nailed Him to the cross, put a crown of thorns on His head, and stabbed His side. Men cannot kill God. So God poured His fire of judgment on His one and only Son! He abandoned Jesus, so now He is never able to leave me or forsake me. I traded places with Him, and so can you.

It is finished!

In your quiet time with Him, He will hear your lamentations, and He will answer them with encouragement. He will pour courage on your soul so you can go out and face a world that is getting more hostile toward Christians every day. But remember, no one and nothing is bigger than our God. So after a quiet time of refreshment…

Bring it on!

Jesus asks, "Do you love me?" (John 21:15). He asks you to show it by feeding His sheep. Out of your belly will flow rivers of living water. The Holy Spirit will never leave you and will always guide you.

You have arrived…

Only to crash. What happened? The addiction comes back stronger. It seems like you are running on empty, and you have nothing to give. What happened to the rivers of living water? They seem out of sight. Your faith that moves mountains is still intact, but without His love, you amount to nothing. You did not answer the question, "Do you love me?" How far will you go to please a lover? Will rejections matter? Will you empty your savings for a diamond ring? Even if ten men reject you, looking into His eyes for hours will fill your love tank. His love rejects rejection and gives life to victory. Victory leaves the house after a while, and His love alone is all you need.

When you see a lovely lady and your infatuation in-toxicates you, do you need the advice to spend time with her? No. How many sermons have you heard about the importance of spending time with the Lord? You do it for a bit, and the visible gives way to the invisible. He has to love you first and removes every visual comfort in your life. Samuel's first book reveals what God has done to David to become the man after God's own heart. His love comes with great power to slay giants in the old days and cast out demons today. The joy of the battle's outcome will fade away, but that alone time with Him will make your heart want more of His heart every day.

When David was relaxing from the fights, he needed love. He looked at a woman bathing and slept with her and killed her husband. What was God's response? He said He could have given David more love! My answer would be, "What is wrong with you?" But I am receiving power to become more like Jesus. God goes after the root cause to build David into a future psalmist fully dedicated to the Lover of His soul.

"Do you love me?" He says. Me? Not the ministry or what He can do for you and in you and through you. "Do you love me?" You can only love Jesus well when you know that He first loved you and died for you. When that sinks in after hearing and hearing the good news, time alone with Him becomes as natural as the first days of an intoxicating infatuation—except this one will never end. How did David become a man after God's own heart?

Jesse, David's dad, ignored him. He preferred his other children. When the prophet Samuel came to visit, the future king was uninvited. David did not care. He was feeding the sheep because he loved the Shepherd who led him to the green pasture. He was practicing his talent on bears and lions. But wait! A teenager needs his father's affection. He loved the Shepherd and enjoyed spending time with Him. God took away a loving family so the tangible comfort would give way to the invisible divine need.

God brought Jesse into David's destiny. Now Jesse is sending David to the victory of all victories. He sent him to his brothers with some food. Someone else will take care of the sheep. Sure, God uses anyone. The focus is on Him, not on the family. David did not apply some rules of boundaries to distance himself from harmful people like his dad. No, he obeyed his dad because His Daddy God said so at that time. The same God will have different approaches for different situations.

There is no formula—only a living relationship. The shepherd's next job after the anointing is Uber Eats delivery. Is that the anointing? Where is the glory? Who cares? David wants to be with his King of kings. Running after animals, lying on the grass, fishing in still waters, or delivering cheesy bread does not matter. His life partner only matters. The valley of Elah lies between two mountains, David's people on one and the enemy on the other. Caught in the middle, David volunteered for a fight no one dared to take on. He was the only one sizing up the God of Israel instead of his own height versus a 10-foot muscle maniac with armor of steel. The Lord helped David with lions and bears. David had seen the goodness of God in the land of the living before. What is Goliath to the Maker of mountains and valleys? He's smaller than a mustard seed (1 Samuel 17:1–58).

David sized up his ally and strategically walked toward his enemy for a full victory. His people got more courageous, invaded enemy territories, and fought left and right to continue all the way. David left for another delivery. What? With his now uniquely acquired giant-slaying skills, he had five stones. Goliath had four big brothers. David was getting ready to finish the entire thing. He carried five stones in his bag. The Lover of his soul asked for a strange delivery that Jesse's son could not understand at the moment. He had to quickly use his moral compass.

If he goes into an honest strategy mode, it makes no sense to leave a battle behind to bury some dude's head so far away. Take the head of Goliath, and walk 17 miles to a hill that will be known in the future as Golgotha. The question is not "Do you understand me?" The problem is the same today and yesterday. The question is, "Do you love me?" David had no idea at that time in the heat of the battle that Jesus would crush Satan's head on Golgotha. That's where he had to bury Goliath's head. He was preparing the messianic covenant.

While he was relaxing by still waters, David knew what it was all about as he penned Psalm 22. Jesus crushed the head of Satan on the cross so we can all step into the green, peaceful pastures with God our Shepherd in Psalm 23. The 17-mile trip with the dude's head smelling real bad for a long time to satisfy God's love makes sense now. The moral strategy gives us peace when we process all the facts. We need a "now" Word from our divine eternity Partner in the heat of the battle, a moral compass. It does not have to make immediate sense. We love Him and trust Him that He has the best for us or nothing. The morality strategy consists of spending time thrilled with His Word, treasuring and chewing each one, remembering every moment day and night.

Before He asks us to feed His sheep, He provides us with His Word, which is way more nutritious than bread for our souls, spirits, and bodies. Only then can we become a tree replanted in Eden, never dropping a leaf—always in blossom. All that really matters in life are moments with Him. Like two lovers in a Michelin star restaurant with a rotating view of the entire city from the ninety-fifth floor, part of the food makes it to the bathroom the next day. The picture becomes the same after 360 degrees. Their eyes are fixed on each other, and the conversation does not have a dull moment. They're living life, an abundant life. An overflow of divine love to bless others after a secret devotion behind closed doors reaches a delighted state. Unforgettable! Now that you are filled with His glory, you are ready to come out of your closet prayer and overflow with blessings to other people.

CHAPTER 11

BUILD OTHERS UP

Let not your heart be troubled!

You open the door of your prayer closet, and the TV is screaming fear. The fridge has ice cream for comfort. The attack on your soul and immune system has started. It will get worse. Are you ready to feed the sheep that Jesus entrusted you with?

First, take a chill pill. Breathe—deep breath.

You have stayed seated for a while in your prayer closet in the previous chapter. What a fantastic time with the Lord! How long? Until you receive word from Him that answers your deepest needs. It could take ten minutes, and it could take six hours. You can do it in the morning or at night. But it has to be as natural as two lovers getting together. You can't wait to see Him.

There are twenty-four hours in each day and seven days a week. You have eight hours to sleep, twelve hours to work, two hours for friends and family, and two hours for the Lord. There is one day for rest and six days for work. There is a beautiful rhythm in a Jewish biblical calendar. The rhythm of grace is unforced. Please don't go to a miracle worker and say it is the Sabbath; stop doing miracles. The other end of the spectrum is to work nonstop, burn out, and lose on spending time with the Lord and your loved ones.

A well-known pastor cheated on his wife. I love him and his church, so I will refrain from mentioning his name. He has done so much for the kingdom and preached to millions worldwide. They asked him why. He said he was running on empty. He had not spent quiet time alone with the Lord for three years. Preparing a message does not count. He had to hear specific daily words for him only and enjoy that divine romance with the Lover of his soul. There is no substitute, and without it, he, you, and I amount to nothing. Should there be grace for him? Yes. In the future, God will amazingly use him. Should he be fired from his job? Absolutely! Your wife, friends, and coworkers are not Jesus. They deserve fruit, and God makes sure they will get that fruit. There is no grape without the Vine. So stay connected to the Vine in a daily quiet time. If not, you will find it difficult to build yourself and others up, 100 percent guaranteed. How can you charge up your spiritual batteries to 100 percent? How can you build up others instead?

Get some olive oil or any type of oil you have in the kitchen. Pray this over it to consecrate it: "I ask you, Lord, to anoint it in the name of Jesus. Let this oil be set

apart for Your purposes to heal the sick and break any
yoke of bondage." You can put a tiny bit on your forehead
or anyone who is sick. Let's see what happens after Samuel anointed David with oil. The Spirit came with power
on David from that day forward. What was his immediate
victory?

Saul needed some comfort after being tormented by
an evil spirit. He inquired about who could play some
music for him. How did David enter the palace? Did
he go empty-handed? Jesse took a donkey loaded with
bread, a jug of wine, and a young goat (1 Samuel 16:20–
21, MSG). Bread and wine represent the body and blood
of Christ. Jesus entered Jerusalem on a donkey. What a
beautiful shadow of the donkey's load of the New Testament in the Old Testament. David did not leave empty-handed. He was loaded with bread and wine. God's
yoke is easy, and His burden is light.

The same way Jesus was casting demons, David
approached Saul playing the harp. Saul got refreshed, and
the evil spirit left him. So much power lies in the anointing oil to reveal Christ riding on a donkey and then cast
out demons. Oil is produced by crushing olives. For the
bread and the wine, Jesus said to eat and drink to remember Him. David, the son of Jesse of Bethlehem, was a
type of Christ. After David defeated Goliath, Saul forgot
who David was. He was told before about the musician
son of Jesse. He received deliverance with wine and
bread. Yet he forgot and had to ask his people and David

whose son he was. He did not remember the bread and the wine, and Saul's end had begun. Many believers fall sick and die the same today because they don't discern the bread and the wine.

David told Saul, "I am the son of your servant Jesse the Bethlehemite" (1 Samuel 17:58, NKJV). Saul could care less. At the exact moment when David finished that last sentence introducing himself, the soul of David was bonded to the soul of Jonathan, son of Saul. David is a type of Christ from Bethlehem. Powerful words created a strong friendship instantly.

What is the main benefit of evangelism? God can send angels or DVDs from heaven, declaring Jesus's death and resurrection and pointing people to Christ. As Jesus lives in me and when I tell others about the One born in a manger in Bethlehem, strong bonds form. In the Garden of Eden, God spoke to a sinless man that it was not suitable for him to be alone. So He created an innocent woman for Adam to bond with and fill the earth. Sin entered the world, and they both become guilty. With Christ, there is a human relationship ignited by the Son of David from Bethlehem, more vital than a love between a man and a woman—kingdom friendship!

Always tune to His voice. You want to build up others. You will hurt them even if you mean well without live divine guidance. You can look up scripture and rely on good old advice or laws and commandments. You can pull up all the "Do Nots." Step away from the tree of good and evil, and follow the unforced rhythms of grace. Under the new covenant, God will be merciful to our unrighteousness, sins, and lawless deeds. He will not remember any of them!

This is how you build up others: heal them, comfort them, and cast out demons. Prayer is not only about comfort or a spa with waterfalls and classical music. Prayer has the authority to evict demons and heal the sick. Prayer moves mountains and shakes the ground. After the house of evil is foreclosed by the blood of Christ, there is no more need for the law. Peace, love, joy, self-control, kindness, and gentleness will build excellent relationships. These chainsaws of love will cut the head off the bear of low self-esteem. Revival will arise. Build others with those tools made by the Spirit. Above all, point them to the King of kings who entered Jerusalem on a donkey. King Jesus.

Run to Jesus only, and live. That is how you build others up with grace. You only preach Jesus and Him crucified. You open Scripture and see Jesus on so many pages from Genesis to Revelation. Jesus hid as a random traveler from the distressed couple on the road to Emmaus and showed them Himself in Scripture. They were refreshed. Follow Him.

The law on two tablets cannot save you. It is holy. Grace completes the law by enabling you to be lawful and exceed its expectation with extraordinary generosity and love toward others. Reveal the beauty of redemption from a million perspectives hidden in the Word. And watch! Oh, watch your people getting transformed from glory to glory without any human under a pure divine intervention!

When you step out in faith to reach a broken world, your physical eyes will be in shock. You have to open your spiritual eyes that were trained earlier in your prayer closet. You will see an army of angels supporting you. And in the most challenging moments, the ravens will not feed you. Jesus Himself will cook for you (1 Kings 19:7). The angel of the Lord in the Old Testament refers to Jesus before His incarnation.

How beautiful is the body of Christ—blameless without any blemish, ready for the big wedding up in the clouds when the trumpet will soon sound. In the meantime, the world is getting darker. How do you stockpile heavenly treasures with all these attacks against you?

CHAPTER 12

STOCKPILE HEAVENLY TREASURES

You are here! You have hit the golden jackpot for heavenly treasure 777. Seven is the number of completion, resting in God, while six ushers in human effort.

A lonely night turns into an affair that tears you apart. You tried to apply all the advice you learned from self-help books, but you failed. First six. You compromise in a business deal when times are tough. You looked at the plaque carved in stone, "In business to glorify God." Second six. Your best friend, a brother in Christ, has this annoying habit. He trusted you for years, but your emotions win, and you gossip—third six. No one trusts you now. You are saved by grace yet cursed under the law. A heavenly treasure is when your lifestyle matches your conviction. If it is easy, the big shots would have done it. Paul would not have confessed that he still does what he does not want to do (Romans 7:15, TPT). This is the guy that Jesus knocked off his horse and spoke to.

How would you add to your life everything you want and need? Above all, run nonstop after the righteousness that comes from Jesus, not human effort. Everything you want and need comes with it (Matthew 6:33, TPT). How do you run after *His* righteousness? You have three sixes to reverse. Paul did it in Romans 12 after he struggled in Chapter 7 (Romans 12:1, TPT), and so can you. Suppose you have made mistakes in the past. In that case, God will bring a great future with high-quality friends, prosperity, and youth renewal. The slot machine is rolling slowly.

Joshua 6 (AMP). Matthew 6 (TPT). John 6 (TPT). Joshua 6 (AMP).

It is a lockdown in Jericho. The first verse of the sixth chapter of Joshua screams, "Gates barred!" No one went out, and no one came in. The dominion in that city was strong. No man can stand against it. Two options are under the sixth term: defeat or fight in vain. God could not wait. He entered the second verse of the sixth chapter and spoke to Joshua. "See I have given Jericho into your hand" (Joshua 6:2, NKJV). See? Can't you see the lockdown? He wanted Joshua to see the victory before the victory and react with singing.

Everyone screamed, "It is a dark winter." Whose vote count is in your eyes? The fact that doors are barred? Everyone or the One? Joshua did not go to his best buddies. He did not call for a meeting to strategize. He opened his ears and received gifts from the Lover of his Soul, the Maker of heaven and earth. Who can stand against Him?

What wall is more significant than Him? What closed door can He not break open? Joshua saw. Do you see it?

Joshua fought giants in the past. His buddy said, "Come on, trust in the Lord. We can knock 'em dead again." God did it in the past, and He will be faithful again. But He will use a different method. So it is vital to tune in to what Abba Father is doing at this moment, or you might miss it.

In the third verse of the sixth chapter of Joshua's book, God broke human effort in two. Six was broken in half. All the armed men for six days did not fight at all. They marched peacefully around the city. The human effort was muted for six days.

But on the seventh day, the day of rest in the Lord, they marched around the city seven times. What did the preachers do? They blew the trumpets made of rams' horns. The rams were sacrifices to God. Did they preach how evil Jericho is? Nope. Did they debate who is more evil than whom? Nope. They proclaimed loudly and clearly the sound of a dead sacrifice that shadows the cross. Just the shadow brought the walls of evil down. We have the real deal. How much more victory will we experience?

An intense moment of temptation arises that we can no longer see the cross or its shadow. It seems there is no way out as we get more self-occupied. The walls look prominent and tall. The world tells us to talk it out with a friend or a therapist. Around a gigantic stronghold, God instructed His people to remain silent for a while. That silence turns a natural reaction into calm thoughts that allow divine intervention. The Holy Spirit will remind us to sound the horn of salvation and wear the robe of righteousness as a gift from Christ, no matter how dirty we are.

At this very moment, ignore the snake's whisper that you are a hypocrite. Don't listen to it. Open your mouth and declare this:

> I am pure in Christ without any blemishes since we traded places. He is naked on the cross while I am clothed with goodness and mercy all my life. I am rich because He became poor for me. I am joyful because He took my place of shame.

Say it. Repeat it daily. Say it when tempted and in the middle of sinning. Say it until it speaks you into the likeness of Jesus—perfect in every way. The wall of your strongholds will crumble like Jericho when the cry of His redemption hits it hard. You will become so good! So good! The desire to do the things you don't want to do will disappear. Who struggled to endure? Not you. All the glory to Jesus! You just relax and speak loud and well of His gift of righteousness. Every blessing will hunt you down. God's ears love the sound of grace.

THE FIRST SIX TURNS INTO A SEVEN MATTHEW 6 (TPT)

Where is your treasure? Open your bank app or bank website. What do you spend money on? Candy makes your teeth decay, beauty supplies make you look younger, a big house makes you clean more and steals your time. I love candy, I use creams on my face to stay hydrated, and I have a big place. Nothing is wrong with that. The sixth chapter of Matthew does not tell us not to have stuff. This has been preached a million times, and it is not in Scripture. It is a dead tradition of broken poetry that changed no one's life. The key is "Do not store up yourselves treasures on earth" (Matthew 6:19, NASB). Those words in the Passion Translation say, "Don't keep hoarding for yourselves earthly treasures" (Matthew 6:19, TPT). Notice the word *hoarding*. You are blessed to be a blessing. You have a big house, so throw a big party to tell people about Jesus. You have some nice creams to keep you young, so have a TV show that talks about Jesus and attracts nonbelievers. You have a jet, so book evangelistic campaigns around the globe back to back. Let's get to work and preach the gospel to all nations until Jesus comes back.

In the Lord's prayer, heaven comes to earth. So investing in heavenly treasures is not far away from the land. They are on the ground. Divine gems are eternal realities present here and now. While savings are eaten by inflation, it is good to have small emergency short-term savings. Investments grow. Invest in God's Word through the local church and missions to the world. Imagine your mansion in heaven filled with people who you have contributed to one way or the other so they can take the next step with Jesus. Do you think God's hand will short-change you on earth? I double triple dare you. Test Him in this area, and He will open the floodgates of blessings on you. You will not only have more money in the bank, but there will be fewer incidents that break the bank. You will have not only friendships that use you but angel investors who fuel your business. Floods of blessings! Get ready! Your cups will overflow, and your containers cannot contain them. You will bless everyone around you.

Human effort tells you to save. Every part of your flesh tells you to keep more for more rainy days. The second six of 666 is where you will be able to function, buy, and sell. Divine rest tells you to invest in God's work and watch Him bless your socks off on earth and in heaven.

THE SECOND SIX TURNS INTO A SEVEN. JOHN 6 (TPT)

John 6:66 is about turning away from the communion truth. This was a truth hard to swallow—literally. They listened to the sermon and experienced the miracle of feeding 5,000 people with five loaves. That was not enough to graduate to the seventh grade. They remained at John 6:66, and no account of their future was ever recorded. Why is turning the third six into a seven hard to swallow?

The first invitation to the holy communion to the 5,000 happened in John 6:53 (TPT): "Eat the body of the Son of Man and drink his blood." The crowd was disgusted, and the majority left. They were warned—this was not a suggestion. Without it, there is no eternal life. Still, they left. The rest stayed. There was no explanation for the people in John 6 whether they have to eat his actual body or not. Later on, Jesus expanded on that truth with matzo bread and wine. Why did He not fully reveal the communion elements that represent His body and blood? To display the heart of the miracle recipient. If some said, "Jesus, what do you mean?" He could have said, "I will tell you when you are ready to hear it." No, they did not do that. They left the hand that fed them and insulted Him. In John 6:66, He is now just another man in their human eyes with miracles going in the wrong direction about eating flesh and blood.

Do you want the benefit or the Maker? Jesus will not be a means to an end. He does not keep a record of wrongs. He is love, and there is no condemnation for those in Him. But if your heart is not for Him and you do not desire to eat in communion with Him, there is no salvation. He is the truth, the way, and the life. No one comes to the Father except through Him. Everyone who wants to come is welcome. So come, and stay. Eat and drink, following His way. Break the bread that is His body, and partake. Drink the wine that is His blood and be protected now and forever.

In the third chapter of this book, I revealed that you will have no sick days because of communion. By His stripes, you are healed. The broken bread is for your healing. But look at Him in Scripture. You will become like Him. There is more healing for your body and brain. You will get younger like an eagle, and your mind will get sharper and produce rare works of art and science. Only your words and beliefs can limit a limitless God. Nothing and no one else can stand against Him. He is a gentleman—if you don't want it, you will not get it.

THE THIRD SIX TURNS INTO A SEVEN.

Go!

You are free from strongholds that are meant to destroy you!

Go!

You stockpile heavenly treasures by funding those who preach the gospel!

Go!

Jesus remains the center of your life even when it does not make sense!